Published by: Boulder Press, P.O. Box 2001, Boulder, CO 80305
Photography and Text © 2010 Mike Barton

Individual prints may be purchased directly from the photographer: cell phone 720 934-4322.
Photographer's website: www.mikebartonphoto.com.

Photo credits: Pg. 38-39 Nubs Nob, Pg. 84 Petoskey Area Visitors Bureau, Pg. 120 Bay Harbor Foundation.
Editors: David L. Miles and Ruth Shilling. Thanks to Ryan Watts for the tour of Harbor Springs. Go State!

Library of Congress Control Number: 2009913489
ISBN 13: 978-0-9801024-5-1
ISBN 10: 0-9801024-5-6
First Printing: 2010
Printed in China

Harbor Springs Petoskey and Bay View

photography and text by Mike Barton

with Mary Agria and Stafford C. Smith

BOULDER PRESS

RICHARD,
ENJOY !!
M. BARTON
2010

CONTENTS

Sunset over Pine River and Lake Michigan from my parent's deck in Charlevoix. As my father looked out over this wonderful scene while enjoying a before-dinner cocktail, he would often quip, "Too bad we don't have a view."

DEDICATED TO MY FATHER

Graham Barton was a gifted engineer and businessman, loving husband, father, grandfather, brother, uncle and friend. He died on August 23, 2009 in Charlevoix the Beautiful.

He loved "Up North" Michigan and spent nineteen wonderful summers in Charlevoix. For many years, he would answer the phone with an exhilarating "Charlevoix the Beautiful!" And if you ever came through the Pine River channel that connects Lake Michigan to Round Lake, he was probably the guy standing high on his deck waving. That was what Graham was about; he was a people person.

Graham was one of few people who rooted for both Michigan State and Michigan because his two sons graduated from one or the other. But deep down, I know he was a Michigan State man.

He was a man of many passions to which he devoted his time and energy. From restoring military vehicles to hunting to preparing for his grandsons' annual visit to Charlevoix, Graham did everything with total enthusiasm. He loved being a Marine and there was no better example of "Once a Marine, Always a Marine."

Graham lived well, traveled the world dozens of times and touched many lives. He was kind-hearted, entertaining, generous and just an all around good guy. We are all richer to have known him and, for that, we are very grateful.

This 1931 Model A Ford was built long after most of the cottages in Bay View were constructed.

FOREWORD

Mike Barton's book is a beautiful, long-overdue tribute in text and image to Northern Michigan's Little Traverse Bay. From the incredible "Brigadoon" known as Bay View, to the Gaslight heart of Petoskey and the glittering deep water anchorage of Harbor Springs – the communities ringing Little Traverse Bay are the stuff of legends. Hemingway called the area home. Anyone who has experienced the four-season lifestyle the region has to offer, visitors and locals alike, will never forget it. Mike lovingly captures the charm of gingerbread architecture, tree-lined shopping districts, historic inns, the natural beauty of the Bay and traditional resort living at its best.

This book makes a wonderful guide to both classic landmarks like the Bay View Encampment and "hidden gems" like the St. Francis Solano Mission and Bear River Pavilion in Petoskey or the "Tunnel of Trees" from Harbor Springs to Cross Village. Architectural photographs become precious resources for tourists and locals alike as they track down historic sites. These are must-visits for their beauty, unique ambiance or contributions to the life of the area. Sunsets, the Bay in its many moods, intimate "pocket" gardens, woodland trails, and beaches imprint themselves on our senses and memories. From fudge to the festivals, the book's images remind us why the region captures hearts and imaginations for generation after generation. Settle down in one of those wooden beach chairs, keep a bucket handy for Petoskey Stones and enjoy.

Mary Agria 2009
A thirty-five year Northern Michigan summer resident, Bay View author Mary Agria's best-selling novel Time in a Garden was inspired by the unique beauty and sense of community of Little Traverse Bay. She has gone on to celebrate the special character of the region and small town living in her novels Vox Humana: The Human Voice, In Transit and the Community of Scholars.

A VISIT WITH STAFFORD

Janice and I met Mike Barton for Sunday Brunch at the Bay View Inn and he asked me to write about my experiences here and what this area means to me. Well, the photos in this book go a long way in telling the story. This region has been a resort area for summer visitors since the 1870s and is now the ski capital of the Midwest. I am happy to be part of this resort tradition through Stafford's Hospitality. My properties are a vital part of each community in maintaining the American Heritage of small, intimate towns.

I was born in Petoskey by accident. My grandfather purchased a cottage in Petoskey in 1919 and my family had the privilege to spend the month of July here. As my dad was packing up to return to Albion, my hometown, my mother informed him that she would be giving birth a little sooner than planned. An Indian child and I initiated the new obstetrics wing of Lockwood Hospital that day.

Following my freshman year at Northwestern in 1957, I came to Petoskey to live with my Aunt Mary and attend Albion summer college in Bay View. She would often take me to Sunday dinner at the Bay View Inn where I met the owner Dr. Roy Heath. He offered me a job and that began my career in the hotel business. I returned each summer as the head desk clerk.

1960 was a fateful summer. Upon my college graduation, Dr. Heath asked me to return to the Inn for one more summer as the general manager. His duties at

Northern Michigan University had expanded, making it difficult for him to be at the Inn for the whole summer.

Janice Johnson, a friend of the chef, was hired to come to the Inn as the dining room hostess. Job applications at that time required photos and when Dr. Heath forwarded Janice's application to me, I promptly put her photo in my billfold. It's still there. By the end of the summer, we knew that we would marry just as soon as Janice graduated from college in June.

During the winter season of 1960 I became the assistant manager of the Perry Hotel; however, it was sold in April. I was suddenly out of a job. Being unemployed with a wedding date just a few months away, I needed to find work to show Janice's mother that I could support her daughter. I knew the Bay View Inn was up for sale and did a little research and found that Dr. Heath had had no viable offers for its purchase. I called him to see if he would want me to run the Inn again for him that summer. He said, "Come up to see me." I ended up buying the Inn from him at the ripe old age of twenty-two. That was the beginning of Stafford's Hospitality.

Stafford C. Smith 2009
Owner of Stafford's Bay View Inn and the Perry Hotel in Petoskey, the Weathervane Restaurant in Charlevoix and the Pier Restaurant in Harbor Springs.

Perched high on a ridge, this 1887 Bay View cottage is a popular subject for artists and photographers.

INTRODUCTION

Circling the shores of Little Traverse Bay, the towns of Harbor Springs, Petoskey and Bay View stand out like sparkling diamonds. Little Traverse Bay is a beautiful bay off Lake Michigan roughly 170 feet deep at the "tip of mitt." Rich in history, natural beauty, soothing solitude and unique charm, these communities have drawn people to this area since the horse and buggy days.

For centuries, the shores of Lake Michigan near Little Traverse Bay had been the home of Native Americans. When European settlers arrived in the mid-1800s, they named the area Little Traverse and the territory gently began to develop.

With the advancement of trains and lake steamships in the late-1800s, summer visitors from the hot, muggy and smoke-filled industrial cities soon discovered the fresh air around Little Traverse Bay. Not only could asthma and hay fever sufferers find instant relief, they could also escape the heat and enjoy scenic views, clean water, spectacular sailing, nature areas, resort atmosphere and beautiful sunsets that made it a compelling summer retreat. "A Look Around Little Traverse Bay" is a book by Candace Fitzsimons that explores the rich history of this region.

Ernest Hemingway spent many summers of his youth fishing, sailing and exploring the forests around the Little Traverse Bay area and later wrote stories about his experiences. In letter to a friend, he called this area "a priceless place" because of the great northern air and atmosphere, feeling of freedom and beautiful country.

Today, people come to Little Traverse Bay for many of the same reasons they had generations ago and can't seem to get enough of it. The small town feel, friendly people, recreational activities and beautiful setting are just some of its alluring qualities. And the smell of

homemade fudge still infiltrates the downtown areas as it did over a century ago.

Sheltered along the north shore of Little Traverse Bay is the picturesque village of Harbor Springs. Founded over a century ago, Harbor Springs still has that small town charm, deep blue harbor and unparalleled natural beauty.

Directly across the bay from Harbor Springs is Petoskey with a historic downtown Gaslight District lined by colorful turn-of-the-century brick buildings and gas lights. The city also has a long tree-shaded grassy park and a beautiful waterfront park for those who choose to relax and put up their feet.

Next door to Petoskey is Bay View, an elegant summer resort association set among beech and oak trees on a natural terrace that cascades down to the shoreline. The maze of tree-lined neighborhoods are filled with Victorian cottages, ranging from modest to extremely ornate. The site was originally a Methodist camp and independent Chautauqua in the late 1800s.

Harbor Springs, Petoskey and Bay View are connected by The Little Traverse Wheelway, a 26-mile paved multi-purpose trail that hugs the shoreline with waterfront parks, wide open beaches and incredible panoramic views. The trail starts north of Charlevoix the Beautiful, a charming town with magical appeal that overlooks a great harbor filled with sailboats and yachts. The Wheelway passes through the luxury yacht community of Bay Harbor before passing through Petoskey's Bayfront Park, Bay View's shoreline and Petoskey State Park. The last little section of the trail, with a few alternative routes, winds its way through the woods to Harbor Springs.

If you feel like exploring a little more inland, you can take a ride to Boyne City on the east end of Lake Charlevoix. On the way there, you will pass along Walloon Lake where Ernest Hemingway's family had a summer cottage. Horton Bay, down the road from

Boyne City, is another Hemingway hangout and a step back in history that shouldn't be missed.

A good day-trip is to visit the famous Mackinac Island, about 50 miles northeast of Petoskey. The island appears to have stopped in time, a place where bicycles and horses rule the roads. It's always fun to check out the Old World downtown, timeless 1887 Grand Hotel and historic Fort Mackinac.

In the fall, the scenic drive between Harbor Springs and Cross Village is a must see. The road narrows and winds through a cathedral of trees – an image you only see in travel magazines. This awesome stretch of road along Lake Michigan is called the "Tunnel of Trees."

Whether you choose to walk along the shores searching for Petoskey Stones, stroll through the delightful downtowns, enjoy an array of outdoor activities or just take in the incredible splendor of Little Traverse Bay, it is definitely worth making a trip "Up North" to experience the good life.

LEFT: The west end corner of charming but upscale Main Street in downtown Harbor Springs.

BELOW: The July Fourth Independence Day parade in Harbor Springs stretches for several blocks as over 100 entrants wind down Main Street then head up Bay Street.

One of the many homes along the Wequetonsing shoreline in Harbor Springs.

You can find something for everyone at Grandpa Shorter's Gifts in Petoskey's Gaslight District, a popular destination for tourists. The son of Chief Petosegay purchased the souvenir shop in 1880.

RIGHT: Many people spend the day at Petoskey's Bayfront Park. The park, located along Little Traverse Bay, features bike paths, ball fields, playgrounds, a marina and is host to many events and activities.

BELOW: The Flatiron building on Howard Street is home to the Flatiron Deli. The building is located right next to Pennsylvania Park and the deli and other establishments open out onto the peaceful park.

Sunset at the Petoskey marina on a warm and calm August evening along Little Traverse Bay

The stillness of the harbor has a calming effect.

HARBOR SPRINGS

Nestled against the steep bluffs along the shores of Little Traverse Bay is the town of Harbor Springs. Thousands of years ago, glaciers carved the deep harbor and grand ridges, creating the natural beauty and endless playground that make Harbor Springs a popular destination.

Native Americans originally settled just north of Harbor Springs around 1700. They called this area Waganakising, meaning "it is bent" in reference to an oddly shaped pine tree that was an eye-catching landmark along the shoreline. European traders just called this area L'Arbre Croche or "Crooked Tree."

The Village of Little Traverse was established in 1858 as trading posts began to appear along the harbor. It became a summer destination for passenger ships and trains in the 1870s and summer resorts at Wequetonsing and Harbor Point quickly formed, making it a playground for Midwestern royalty.

Many well-known wealthy families like the Fords,

Upjohns, Gambles (of Proctor & Gamble), and Offields (of Wrigley Gum) built summer cottages here. The exclusive Harbor Point, situated on a long-thin peninsula that juts out to form the pristine harbor, comes complete with guards and gates. You have to know someone who knows someone and you still might not get in. Wequetonsing is another private colony of spacious summer homes along the waterfront but is mostly accessible to the public.

The town was eventually renamed the Village of Harbor Springs in 1881, a reasonable choice based on the beautiful natural harbor and the gurgling springs in the area.

Today, Harbor Springs has a quaint but upscale downtown near the waterfront, the same scenic beauty and many fairs and festivals. Outdoor enthusiasts can enjoy golf, skiing, biking and sailing or just hang out in one of the downtown parks or beaches and watch glamorous yachts and sailboats skim across the harbor.

OPPOSITE PAGE: Locals and visitors of all ages get a chance to march or ride in the pedestrian part of the Fourth of July parade.

RIGHT: Colorful chairs are lined up along on Main Street hours before the Independence Day parade in anticipation of the most popular event of the year.

BELOW: Proud drivers of spotless and polished vintage cars idle and gas up Bay Street.

LEFT: As another boating season comes to a close, one of the few sailboats remaining in the marina heads out for an early morning trip in the peaceful harbor.

BELOW: It's easy to lose yourself in the gentle reflections along the waterfront.

The Harbor Springs train depot now houses an art gallery and other businesses. Ernest Hemingway and his family often came to Harbor Springs by steamship and then took the train to Walloon Lake where they vacationed in the summer.

The uniquely shaped "Hexagon House" was built in 1892 by Shay locomotive inventor Ephraim Shay near downtown Harbor Springs. The Shay locomotive was designed specifically for the lumber industry and shipped all over the world. Shay was more than just an inventor; he was a Civil War Veteran, physician, schoolteacher, lumberman, civil engineer and railway owner.

This view of Holy Childhood of Jesus Catholic Church was taken from the bluff high above Harbor Springs.

You'll get that "deer in the headlights" look when you visit Deer Park near the Police Station. If you throw apples they will come. Deer Park is administered by the local Police Department.

RIGHT: The Harbor Springs High School steel drum band performs at the annual Holiday Open House on a chilly December evening.

BELOW: One attempt to photograph the Christmas tree at the end of Main Street took place after midnight so that no cars would be parked along the curb. The street was completely clear, but someone unplugged the tree lights.

ABOVE AND RIGHT: More charming holiday scenes along Main Street.

Winter arrives in Wequetonsing.

LEFT AND BELOW: The name Wequetonsing means "harbor of rest." That seems to explain all the chairs lined up along Weque beach.

ABOVE AND OPPOSITE PAGE: Take some time to admire the gorgeous cottages set on manicured lawns along the Wequetonsing waterfront at the east end of Harbor Springs. Signs along the road say "private," but the streets are open to anyone and the residents are very friendly.

Harbor Springs sunset from the bluff.

RIGHT: The Veranda at Harbor Springs is a historical landmark within strolling distance of downtown and the marina. The Inn was built in 1879 in Petoskey and dragged across the ice by horses to where it sits today nestled along Main Street.

BELOW: Built in 1892, Holy Childhood of Jesus Catholic Church dominates the west end of Main Street.

LEFT AND ABOVE: Nub's Nob opened in 1957 with a single chairlift and just three slopes. Back then, a season pass cost only twenty dollars. If you ever wondered where the name came from, the original owner was Nub Sarns.

RIGHT: Nub's Nob now offers 53 ski slopes and trails on three peaks.

BELOW: With a vertical drop of 552 feet spread across 270 acres, Boyne Highlands offers the longest runs and steepest terrain in the area. During the summer, Boyne Highlands hosts the Young American Dinner Theatre, a hand-picked group of young talent from all over the country that has dazzled dinner-theater audiences since 1977.

Street corners come alive as musicians of all kinds entertain during the Street Musique summer concerts around downtown.

Located in what was the original Harbor Springs United States Post Office built in 1908, Howse's Candy Haus produces many different varieties of homemade fudge and other types of candy.

Solitude can be found in the many lush green nature areas located all around Harbor Springs. The slippery boardwalk and gentle Roaring Brook wind through ferns and pines.

ABOVE: You can get everything from sailing flags to books on how to tie boat knots at By the Bay on Main Street. Can a place look any more nautical than this?

LEFT: About a dozen of these sailboats were zipping around the harbor.

ABOVE AND OPPOSITE PAGE: More beautiful homes found in Wequetonsing.

The Little Traverse Lighthouse, built in 1886, is located at the tip of private Harbor Point and can only be photographed from the shore. The fog bell tower in front of the lighthouse was built in 1896.

RIGHT: The Pointer Boat was a water taxi that carried residents between Harbor Springs and Harbor Point from 1930 until 1962. Today, Stafford's Pier Restaurant offers complimentary harbor tours with a taste of history aboard the completely restored Pointer.

BELOW: After several failed attempts, all of which can be blamed on the photographer and his assistant, a young sailor makes his final approach for a photo op.

ABOVE: Main Street is lit up for the holidays.

LEFT: Stafford's Pier Restaurant, the building with the crow's nest just behind the boats, was built on the harbor's original pilings and served as the boathouse for the Pointer Boat until 1962.

RIGHT: The waterfront parks are good places to relax and enjoy views of the harbor.

BELOW: Countryside like this can be found just north of Harbor Springs.

RIGHT AND BELOW: Turkey's Pizza is a Harbor Springs favorite for breakfast and lunch. When you enter the pink building, it's as if you are taken back to the 1950s. The black and white checkered floor and wooden booths only add character. Old photos and antiques including a collection of old-fashioned soda pop bottles fill the walls. Owner Jeff Graham earned the nickname Turkey when his coach told him he walked like a turkey after he sprained both ankles playing football at Harbor Springs High.

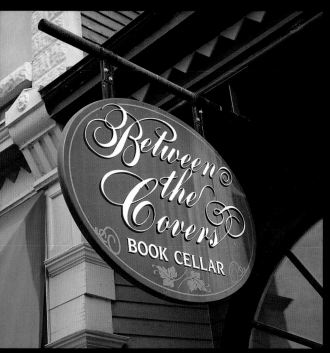

Zorn Park Beach, complete with a changing house and lifeguards, is one of six sandy beaches within a few miles of downtown Harbor Springs.

A 1960 Lincoln Mark V convertible parked in front of the vacant Juilleret's. Owned and operated by the same family for four generations, Juilleret's was Michigan's oldest family-run restaurant dating back to 1895. The homey place closed in 2007.

Not many restaurants can claim that a hit song was composed in their dining room. During the summer of 1923, the popular song, "Sleepy Time Gal" was written and first played inside Juilleret's.

A porch with a view.

A pedestrian tunnel connects Petoskey's Gaslight District to Bayfront Park.

PETOSKEY

Overlooking Little Traverse Bay is Petoskey, a delightful resort town with a people-friendly downtown and waterfront. Petoskey is a year-round community that has been a popular vacation spot for decades, with vacationers returning every year to enjoy the views, play in the water and shop around the bustling downtown. Petoskey inspired Ernest Hemingway's first novel, Torrents of Spring, when he lived there during the winter of 1919-20.

Tourism from passenger trains and steamships played a major role in Petoskey's growth. Thousands of summer visitors came to the area to breath the fresh air and experience the resort atmosphere.

Today, with a population of slightly more than 6,000, Petoskey is the largest community on Little Traverse Bay. The town was named "Petoskey" in honor of Chief Ignatius Petosegay in 1879. Petosegay means "rising sun" or "sunshine of promise" or "light shines through the clouds."

The walkable historic downtown Gaslight District attracts locals and visitor alike as they make their way through an array of art galleries, restaurants, coffee shops, hip cafés and unique local shops. Many stroll or relax in the shady and peaceful Pennsylvania Park that lines the north side of downtown.

Just a short walk away from downtown is Bayfront Park where you can watch the sailboats and yachts, walk the narrow pier to the lighthouse and enjoy the Million Dollar Sunsets.

Scattered along the beaches around Little Traverse Bay you may find a Petoskey Stone, a 350-million-year-old fossilized coral souvenir to take home. The "sunburst" hexagon surfaces make them easy to identify, especially when they are wet.

Visitors take a scenic ride in one of Petoskey's pedicabs.

RIGHT: There are many colorful establishments in the historic Gaslight District in downtown Petoskey.

BELOW: Tucked within a little courtyard behind Symons General Store, Chandler's offers a wonderful and unique outdoor atmosphere.

LEFT AND ABOVE: Many yachts, sailboats and other vessels drop anchor at Petoskey's marina on Little Traverse Bay.

The Petoskey pierhead is a popular place to hang out and have fun during the summer.

Mineral Well Park Pavilion along the Bear River is listed on the National Register of Historic Places.

The Farmers Market in downtown Petoskey is always busy on Friday mornings throughout the summer and early fall. The familiar St. Francis Xavier Church steeple is visible in the background.

When polished or wet, the Petoskey Stone's unique hexagon pattern fully emerges. This collection is from Bailey's Place, located just north of Petoskey, where you can find a wide variety of high quality stones. The Petoskey Stone was named Michigan's state stone in 1965.

Symons General Store is a beacon of the Gaslight District. The red brick structure, built in 1879. is always a treat to browse and features one of the oldest candy counters in Northern Michigan.

Kids enjoy playing in Pennsylvania Park, a beautiful tree-shaded lawn divided by railroad tracks that used to bring trains full of summer visitors from 1873 to 1960. Several establishments open out to the happy park, including Murdick's Fudge where they have been serving since 1887.

RIGHT: Housed in once was the historic Petoskey United Methodist Church, built in 1877, the Crooked Tree Arts Center is home to two art galleries and a large performing arts theatre.

BELOW: It took six years to complete the St. Francis Xavier Church after it was begun in 1903. The bricks were made in Boyne City, shipped to Petoskey by rail and carried to the site by horse and wagon. The steeple can be seen for miles.

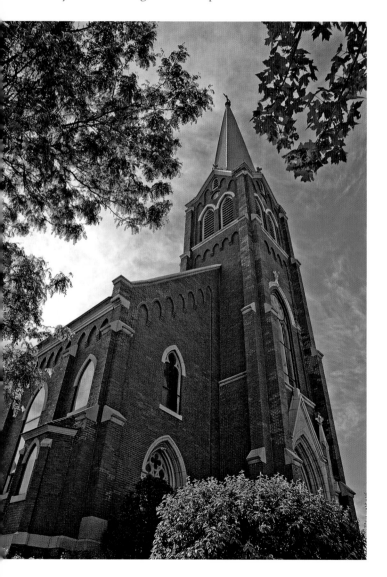

Replicas of the Nina and Pinta, which sailed across the Atlantic with Christopher Columbus in 1492, were docked in Petoskey and open for self-guided tours in July 2009.

LEFT AND BELOW: Built in 1899, Stafford's Perry Hotel is the only one of twenty luxury resort hotels built around the turn of the century that is still open. The elegant hotel with Old World charm sits high on a bluff overlooking Little Traverse Bay. The Perry was also the first brick hotel in Petoskey and back then was advertised as the only fireproof hotel in town.

St. Francis Solano Mission church was built in 1859 and may be the oldest building in Petoskey.

Children flock to the playground at Bayfront Park.

RIGHT: This lifeboat accompanied the John A. Galster, a freighter that served the Petoskey Portland Cement Factory located on the present site of the Bay Harbor resort. The 22-foot steel lifeboat was built in 1925 and has been fully restored.

BELOW: And they say the sun doesn't come out during the winter in Northern Michigan.

Since 1965, Cutler's has been a popular kitchen and home store. With its bright yellow awnings and corner location, Cutler's may be the most recognizable store in the Gaslight District.

Kitty-corner from Culter's, Pappagallo features upscale women's clothing and accessories. The popular store is housed in a building that was constructed in 1900.

Located in a building that dates back to 1907, McLean & Eakin is an independent bookstore with a helpful, friendly and well-read staff.

For more than a century, Murdick's Fudge and Caramel Corn has been a popular spot for locals and tourist alike. Back in the 1920's, the Murdicks used cooling fans to blow the smell of cooking fudge into the street to help bring in customers.

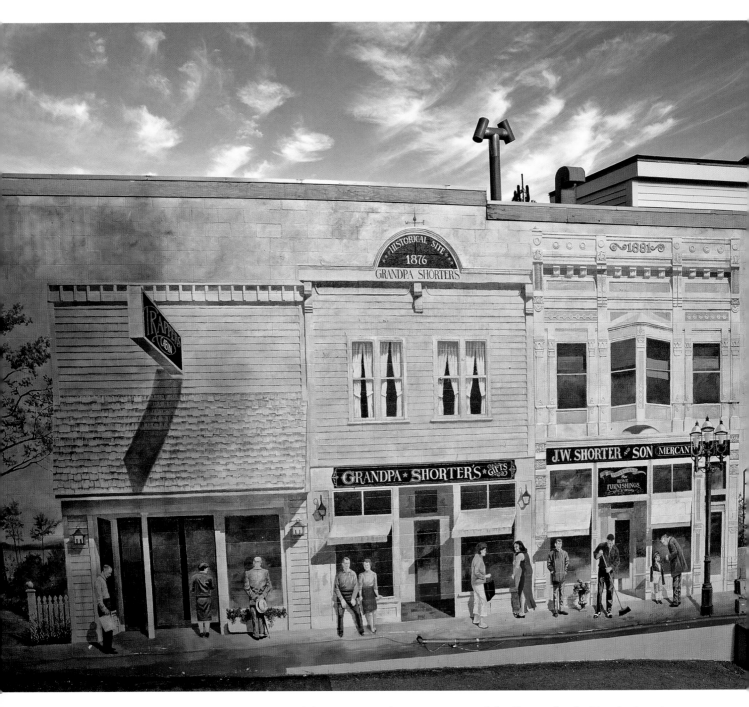

Artist T.L. Dickinson created this mural that represents three generations of the Shorter family. The sky is real.

With an old creaky wooden floor and tin ceiling, Symons General Store is a step back into the past.

ABOVE: Sunset silhouettes help convey the mood near the waterfront. The image on the top right is of Chief Petosegay.

RIGHT: Mya and Mykala speed down the hill at Petoskey's Winter Park in preparation for the 2022 Winter Olympics.

Christmas shopping in the Gaslight District.

BAY VIEW

Bay View is a captivating community set along Little Traverse Bay among beech and oak trees just northeast of Petoskey. Founded as a Methodist camp and summer retreat in 1875, it was originally formed during the Chautauqua movement due to the area's beautiful lakeside location, its healthy summer climate and availability by rail and steamship.

Bay View's terraced land quickly transformed into a summer resort community. Twenty simple cottages and several community buildings were built by 1877. Within ten years, another 125 cottages, a hotel and a chapel were built. Today, Bay View is comprised of more than 440 cottages (the majority of which were built before 1890), two historic inns, thirty community buildings and a post office. The resort is a registered National Historic Landmark.

Bay View is known for its charming Victorian gingerbread-style cottages, some of which are still occupied by descendants of the founding families. Many cottage owners represent third and fourth generations and some families have been a part of Bay View for six generations.

The community is open from May through October when summer cottagers flock to renew old friendships and enjoy the peaceful setting. And it appears nothing much has changed here in the last 100 years.

During the summer, the Bay View Association offers many outstanding concerts, recitals, performing arts,

lectures and educational seminars - all of which are open to the public.

Recreation and sports are an important part of Bay View. Residents can enjoy tennis, swimming, sailing, croquet, lawn bowling and four miles of walking trails in the forest where trolls could live. The "Rec Club" building on the beach is home to many youth programs. Children of all ages can enjoy water sports, athletics, crafts, camping and more.

Bay View has hosted many distinguished speakers such as Helen Keller, William Jennings Bryan and Booker T. Washington. A young Ernest Hemingway also walked the grounds of Bay View. In 1919-1920, while he was living in Petoskey, he often escaped to the privacy of Evelyn Hall, a women's dormitory unoccupied in the winter. During this time he reportedly met his true love who lived in a nearby cottage across from the post office.

LEFT AND BELOW: Tucked among over 440 Victorian cottages, the Terrace Inn is a great location for guests who want to explore the grounds of Bay View. Built in 1911, the Inn has maintained the vintage appeal and relaxing atmosphere of the past. Recent innkeepers have heard so many stories of ghost sightings they were inspired to host a Ghost Hunter weekend where a team of paranormal investigators took guests on a real ghost hunt.

OPPOSITE PAGE: This large cottage is located at the end of an easy to miss cul-de-sac but still gets plenty of attention.

ABOVE AND OPPOSITE PAGE: Just a few of the charming cottages built near the turn of the century.

While living in a Petoskey rooming house during the winter of 1919-1920, Ernest Hemingway occasionally escaped to a small room in Evelyn Hall (1890) in Bay View to get more privacy.

Summer cottagers have headed south for the winter before the snow begins to blanket their resort.

OPPOSITE PAGE AND ABOVE: Many cottages feature gingerbread-trimmed ornamentation.

OPPOSITE PAGE: Lush colorful foliage is just one of many ingredients that gives Bay View its enduring appeal.

RIGHT: Although the bike doesn't appear to be too rideable, it makes the perfect decoration for this charming area.

BELOW: Old-fashioned porches with views like this are common along the Bay View waterfront.

ABOVE AND OPPOSITE PAGE: Sailing, kayaking, games, music, crafts, camping and many other activities are centered around the "Rec Club" and "Sailhouse" on the beach.

OPPOSITE PAGE AND ABOVE: Some of the many white-pillared porches with old-fashioned furniture.

LEFT: A view of Hall Auditorium from the tiny Speaker's Stand. Built in 1876, the Speaker's Stand was Bay View's first community building and was used for outdoor meetings.

BELOW: This foot bridge is hidden along a meandering creek behind the cottages.

LEFT: One of the few porches in Bay View that still has furniture when the leaves change color in mid October.

BELOW: The 2000-seat John M. Hall Auditorium is the "heart of the community" and is home to many of the over 140 programs held each summer at Bay View. The current auditorium was completed and dedicated in 1914 after the original 1887 wooden structure burned down.

Built in 1876, the Horton Bay General Store has changed very little and is still a main gathering place. A young Ernest Hemingway would often canoe across Walloon Lake from his family's cottage and hike about four miles through the forest to visit friends at Horton Bay. Many of his Nick Adams stories take place around this area.

BEYOND LITTLE TRAVERSE BAY

Little Traverse Bay's close proximity to several other wonderful places make it a perfect starting point when you visit Northern Michigan.

You can choose to discover the other harbor towns along Lake Michigan and Lake Charlevoix or head inland to the sleepy and slow-paced villages that look the same as they did 100 years ago. Maybe you want to explore the surrounding forests and wide-open countryside sprinkled with old farms and scenic lakes on the outskirts of town. Or you can hop in a boat where there is almost no limit where you can go including several nearby islands. No one ever seems to be in a hurry around here except for the photographer.

The four seasons transform this area from a boaters paradise to a brilliant autumn for leaf peepers to a winter wonderland for all to enjoy.

ABOVE: One of the many colorful images you will enjoy along "The Little Traverse Wheelway," between Petoskey and Charlevoix.

LEFT: Somewhere on Beach Road, the scenic shortcut out of Harbor Springs back to Petoskey.

On the way to Boyne City from Charlevoix on a chilly fall morning before sunrise, while you were sleeping.

A few minutes later, the clouds parted and the snow ceased.

ABOVE AND RIGHT:
Wintery scenes along the
highway from Charlevoix
to Mancelona.

LEFT AND BELOW: Nestled along the bluffs overlooking Lake Michigan is the village of Good Hart. Rich in Native-American history, Good Hart became a resort destination in the early 1900s. The photos shown here are of Primitive Images and Studio A, both located in the tiny downtown.

ABOVE: This huge birch grove adds a unique texture to the rolling countryside north of Harbor Springs. The trunks look more like aspens than aspens.

LEFT: Hidden in the woods near the road leading to Good Hart.

A foggy and frost-covered October morning at the Boyne City marina.

RIGHT: Almost at the end of the road after a morning exploring the backroads near East Jordan.

BELOW: Sand dunes along Petoskey State Park on the east shore of Little Traverse Bay.

BAY HARBOR

A large cement plant and 100 years of mining operations left a moonscape environment that seemed to turn into a four-season luxury resort community overnight. Several parties teamed up in 1993 to transform this damaged shoreline into a beautiful waterfront playground.

Located just west Petoskey, Bay Harbor has a vibrant setting and a diverse array of events and outdoor festivals. The deep harbor, boat marina, beaches, world-class golf, equestrian club and a village full of boutiques and restaurants make it one of the top harbor resorts in the United States.

The entire history of Bay Harbor can be found in the book "We Did It!" by Samara D. Johnson.

ABOVE: Bay Harbor offers daily summer entertainment.

ABOVE: The covered beach chairs come in handy on windy days along the shoreline.

RIGHT: Perched along Little Traverse Bay, The Inn at Bay Harbor is the resort's centerpiece and is recognized as one of the world's best hotels.

OPPOSITE PAGE: Bay Harbor's biggest weekend during the summer is the Vintage Car & Boat Festival, featuring classic vehicles and wooden boats. Bay Harbor Lake was formed when over 2.5 billion gallons of water from Little Traverse Bay rushed into a former quarry after a restraining barrier was removed.

121

LEFT: The warm glow of sunrise on Water Street in downtown Boyne City.

BELOW: It's autumn when the docks become empty and the leaves in the distance begin to change.

BOYNE CITY

Nestled against rolling hills on the eastern end of Lake Charlevoix about twenty minutes from Petoskey is the community of Boyne City. With miles of lakefront shoreline, a boat marina, world-class golf and a quaint downtown, Boyne City has earned a reputation as a great place to live and visit.

Michigan's first ski resort, Boyne Mountain, is located about eight miles from Boyne City. The property was purchased in 1947 for one dollar.

Before you leave, follow the twisting hilly road north to the village of Horton Bay, a small cluster of buildings including a general store, inns, and several cottages. Ernest Hemingway often came to Horton Bay during his youth to hunt, fish and visit his buddies. It is also where he married his first wife in 1921.

ABOVE: The Boyne Theatre on South Lake Street.

The Boyne City boat marina is situated on the east shore of Lake Charlevoix with easy access to Lake Michigan.

ABOVE: Rush hour. In Charlevoix, it's all about the bridge.

CHARLEVOIX

Charlevoix the Beautiful is a charming harbor town located just fifteen miles west of Petoskey. With many wide open and secluded beaches, golf courses, outdoor events, the "Mushroom Houses," two turn-of-the century summer resort associations and a shopping district with harbor views, Charlevoix has been a summer retreat for generations. Bring your boat shoes.

Many people head to Lake Michigan Beach to check the incoming weather, play in the water, soak up the sun, watch boats come and go or to just enjoy the spectacular sunsets over the great lake.

Boaters from Little Traverse Bay can visit Round Lake harbor in Charlevoix by navigating the short Pine River with its entrance marked by a red lighthouse along the shore of Lake Michigan.

ABOVE: Downtown Charlevoix overlooks the picturesque, almost land-locked Round Lake harbor. The place is pretty enough to just sit back and look at.

RIGHT: This house is the handiwork of legendary stone builder Earl Young. These unique homes are commonly referred to as the "Mushroom Houses of Charlevoix" because of their sweeping rooflines and organic look.

OPPOSITE PAGE: The Charlevoix Lighthouse was repainted to its pre-1968 red in July 2009.

Charlevoix's Bridge Street is usually too crowded of a place to run, but this jogger was out early enough to have the place all to herself.

Located in the heart of Charlevoix's downtown, Sadie's and Jake's is an art café where you can get anything from posters to paninis. The coffee is good too. This lively place has a friendly staff who always make you feel welcome.

ABOVE: When you see this colorful awning, you know you have arrived in Charlevoix.

LEFT: If you want to visit a castle, just head three miles south of Charlevoix to Castle Farms. Built in 1918 by Albert Loeb, it was used until 1924 as a working farm to raise livestock and show off the latest farm equipment. From 1969 to 1999, the Castle was used mainly for rock concerts. In 2005, Castle Farms was completely restored and is now used for weddings, festivals, corporate events and tours.

ABOUT THE PHOTOGRAPHER

Mike Barton is a landscape photographer from Boulder, Colorado. A native of Michigan, Mike moved to sunny California after graduating from Michigan State and began to photograph the Pacific coast. Michigan is a great place to "be from." It wasn't until he moved to Colorado that his passion for photography began to consume more of his time.

In his fourth book, Mike has continued to show off one of the world's best kept secrets, Northern Michigan. During this six-month project, Mike visited "Up North" Michigan five times and took a couple of thousand photos but had to settle on using just over 240 images published in this book.

Many people comment on the vibrant colors that Mike is able to bring out in his photographs. This requires returning to the same place over and over until the light and other conditions are just right. A photo can be taken of the same location on different days and the clouds, colors, waves and reflections can vary dramatically.

To see more of Mike's work, please visit his website: www.mikebartonphoto.com.

In Memory of
My Dog Magic

The word that most people used to describe Magic was "sweet." She had a great life and gave me fifteen wonderful years. Magic died peacefully on January 4, 2009 and is now in puppy heaven.

Magic loved to visit Charlevoix and chase after squirrels she had no chance of catching, run on sugar sand Lake Michigan Beach, play on the huge green lawn near the harbor and vacuum up sweet treats along Bridge Street. She had more frequent flyer miles than most adults.

All of her life, most people thought Magic was a puppy because she was so small. And Magic was definitely a kid magnet and loved the attention.

Magic has also appeared in my other three photo books because she was always there. I have many happy memories of her.

ABOVE: Little Magic was always the center of attention on happy Bridge Street in Charlevoix the Beautiful.

Other "Up North" Books By Mike Barton

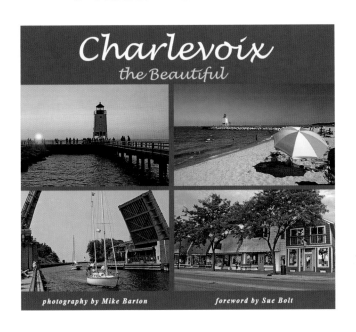